*The decorations which adorn the child's
arms help her to position her head
correctly during the dances.*

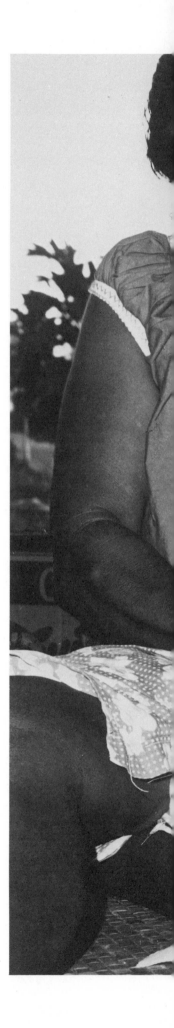

Above: *dancing skirts are made from coconut fronds.*
Right: *relatives of the dancers making headdresses.*

Right: *girls getting ready to dance.*

Above: *a mixed choir provides a rhythmic accompaniment of clapping and singing.*
Right: *the dances evoke powerful emotions at any age.*

216

Left: *the wide skirt worn for the dance te buki accentuates rapid hip movements, while the rest of the body remains static.*
Below: *a child watches the dancing of the opposing team from another village.*
Bottom: *a girl's cheeks are sometimes decorated with grains of coral sand.*

217

Above: *rhythm is sometimes provided by
a circle of men pounding a low wooden box.*
Right: *a dance from Tuvalu.*

220

Right: *decorations are attached to the fingers of the dancer to emphasise each movement.*

Below: *each movement of the team is performed in perfect unison and expresses the words of the song.*

Below: *a te kebae or man's dancing mat is tied with a belt made of his wife's hair.*
Below right: *dancing skirts are blackened with dye and coconut oil makes them shine.*

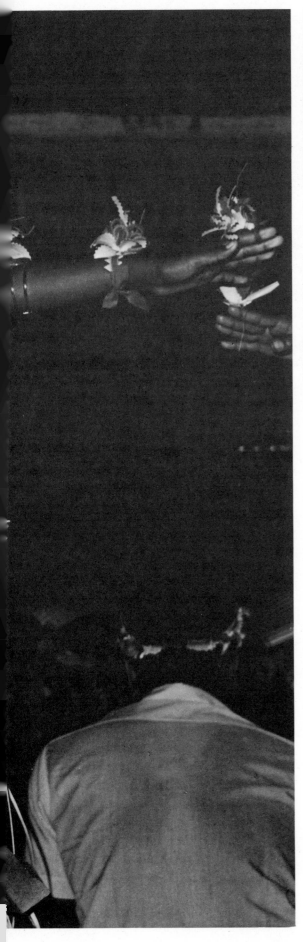

Above: *a child displays remarkable poise as she dances te buki.*
Overleaf: te bino, *or sitting dance is performed by either men or women.*

225

NAREAU'S NATION

A PORTRAIT OF THE GILBERT ISLANDS

TONY WHINCUP

STACEY INTERNATIONAL

First published by Stacey International
1979

© copyright

Stacey International
128 Kensington Church Street,
London W8 4BH

ISBN 0 905743 16 4

Set in Monophoto Photina by
Tradespools Limited, Frome
Printed and bound by
Willsons Printers (Leicester) Limited
Design: Anthony Nelthorpe MSIAD
Cartography: Arka Cartographics Limited

The publishers gratefully acknowledge
permission to quote from the following
books: *Migrations, Myth and Magic from
the Gilbert Islands* by Rosemary Grimble
and published by Routledge and Kegan
Paul; *In the South Seas* by Robert Louis
Stevenson and published by the University
of Hawaii Press; *Astride the Equator* by
Ernest Sabatier and published by Oxford
University Press, Melbourne and *A Pattern
of Islands* by Arthur Grimble and
published by John Murray Limited.

Contents

Foreword

Little perhaps is known of the Gilbert Islands and I understand the difficulty that faces people in far-off places, who, maybe used to the bustling cities of the world, find it hard to visualise a country of coral atolls scattered over many square miles of ocean. Therefore, it is with considerable pleasure that I recommend this publication as a photographic summary, the first of its kind on the Gilbert Islands, of our country, our people and our way of life.

With the advent of Independence, this is a timely record of our traditional life styles and skills. To those who know the Gilbert Islands, I trust that this book will recall happy memories and to others I hope it proves of interest and may even tempt them to visit our shores.

Ieremia Tabai
Chief Minister

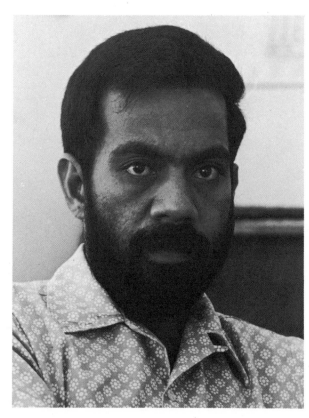

Preface

There is a lack of visual documentation of the Gilbert Islands, a fascinating area where traditional skills still play a vital role in day to day life. The camera is a wonderful catalyst which creates a shared experience between subject and photographer. Where language barriers make communication hard to establish, a camera is seen as a positive demonstration of interest by the Gilbertese. Hospitality is offered and time shared.

I chose black and white film for its clarity. There are beautiful and subtle colours throughout the Islands but, for me, the impact is one of extreme contrasts. Colours disappear against the harsh glare of coral sand or the brilliance of the Pacific sky. The dark-skinned Gilbertese themselves contrast sharply with their sunlit land. Under the broad-leafed breadfruit trees and in the thatched roofed houses deep shadows create a monochrome world.

The photographs have been grouped into chapters, but these areas are not independent of each other. It is not possible to talk of "dancing" to the exclusion of "people", nor of the "sea" without "fishing and canoes".

The Gilbert Islands cannot be adequately captured by surface images, but at best this book documents my impressions of the harmony, skills and ingenuity of the Gilbertese people. It is not, and does not attempt to be, an exhaustive photographic document of all things Gilbertese, but is rather a personal view of occasions, places and people which have intrigued me.

A.W.

Acknowledgements

I would like to thank all those people who helped in so many different ways during the preparation of this book.

In particular I am grateful to the Chief Minister for his Foreword, to the Gilbert Islands Government for their encouragement; to Sheila Harris for her help and suggesting the title of the book; to Dick Ovary for compiling the 'Further Reading' list and to Angus McDonald and John Smith.

I gratefully acknowledge the time, advice and encouragement I have been given by John Pitchford, Howard Van Treese, Roger Harris, Tim Jardine-Brown, Bwere, Gopalakrishnan, Tebaubwebwe Tiata, Tetika Teku, Peter Davies, Kiraata Tekawa and many of the pupils of King George the Fifth and Elaine Bernacchi Schools.

I also wish to express my appreciation of the many people I have photographed who showed me kindness and hospitality.

Lastly I thank my wife, Joan, for her patience and support.

Further reading

BAILEY, Eric. *The Christmas Island Story*, Stacey International, London, 1977

BEAGLEHOLE, J.C. *The Exploration of the Pacific*, 3rd edition, A. & C. Black, London, 1966

CAMERON, J. *John Cameron's Odyssey*, Macmillan, New York, 1923

CARMICHAEL, Peter. *A World of Islands*, text by June Knox-Mawer, Collins, London, 1968

COATES, Austin. *Western Pacific Islands*, (Corona Series), HMSO, London, 1970

CROWL, P.A. and LOVE, E.G. *Seizure of the Gilbert and Marshalls*, US Government Printing Office, Washington, 1955

DAVIDSON, J.W. and SCARR, D. *Pacific Islands Portraits*, Australian National University Press, Canberra, 1970

DAVIS, Captain E.H.M. *Proceedings of H.M.S. 'Royalist', May–August 1892*, edited and reprinted by the Tungavalu Society, Tarawa, 1976

ELLIS, Albert. *Adventuring in Coral Seas*, Angus & Robertson, Sydney, 1936

ELLIS, Albert. *Mid-Pacific Outposts*, Brown and Stewart, Auckland, 1946

ELLIS, Albert and F. *Ocean Island and Nauru*, Angus & Robertson, Sydney, 1935

GILBERT ISLANDS *reports* and Gilbert & ELLICE ISLANDS *reports*, HMSO, London

GRIMBLE, Arthur. *A Pattern of Islands*, John Murray, London, 1952 (Published in USA as *We Chose the Island*)

GRIMBLE, Arthur. *Return to the Islands*, John Murray, London, 1957

GRIMBLE, Rosemary. *Migrations, Myth and Magic from the Gilbert Islands; early writings of Sir Arthur Grimble*, Routledge & Kegan Paul, London, 1972

HADDON, A.C. and HORNELL, J. *Canoes of Oceania*, Bishop Museum Press, Honolulu, 1975

HISTORY OF THE GILBERT ISLANDS. Gilbert Islands University of the South Pacific, Suva, 1978

LEWIS, David. *We, the Navigators*, Reed, Wellington, 1972

MAUDE, H.E. *The Evolution of the Gilbertese boti: an ethno-historical interpretation*, Polynesian Society, Wellington, 1963. Reprinted by University of the South Pacific, 1977

MAUDE, H.E. *Of Islands and Men*, Oxford University Press, Melbourne, 1968

PHELAN, Nancy. *Atoll Holiday*, Angus & Robertson, Sydney, 1958

RICHARDSON, W. *The Epic of Tarawa*, Odhams, London, 1945

SABATIER, Ernest. *Astride the Equator*, translated from the French by Ursula Nixon. Oxford University Press, Melbourne, 1978

SHERROD, Robert. *Tarawa: the story of a battle*. Duell Sloane and Pearce, New York, 1941

SIERS, James. *Taratai*, Millwood Press, Wellington, 1977

SILVERMAN, Martin Gary. *Disconcerting Issue*, University of Chicago Press, Chicago, 1971

STEVENSON, Robert Louis. *In the South Seas*, University of Hawaii Press, London, 1971

TEWAREKA, Tentoa. *These are the Gilberts*, Tarawa Teachers' College, Tarawa, 1976

WARD, E.V. *Sailing directions . . . Gilbert Islands*. Government Printer, Tarawa, 1967. (New edition forthcoming)

WILKES, C. *Narrative of the US Exploring Expedition 1838–1842*, Gregg Press, New York, 1970

See also: Atoll Research Bulletins, Pacific Science Board, Washington; Journal of the Polynesian Society, Wellington, and Journal of Pacific History, Canberra

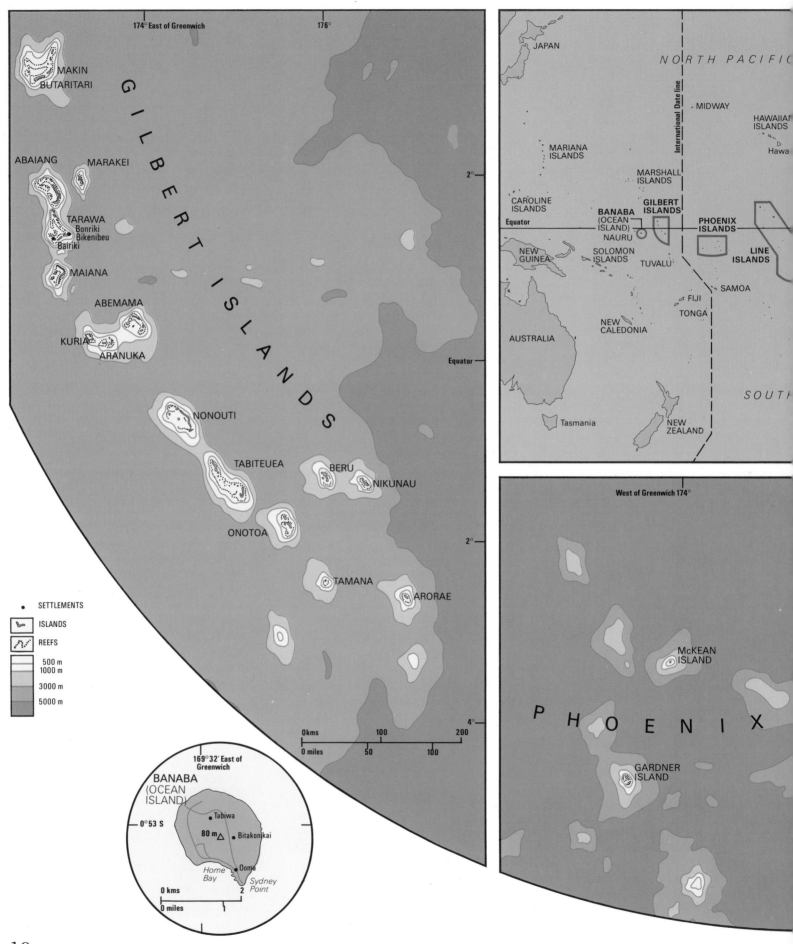

GILBERT ISLANDS

MAKIN
BUTARITARI

174° East of Greenwich
176°

ABAIANG
MARAKEI

TARAWA
Bonriki
Bikenibeu
Bairiki

MAIANA

ABEMAMA

KURIA
ARANUKA

NONOUTI

TABITEUEA
BERU
NIKUNAU

ONOTOA

TAMANA
ARORAE

2°

Equator

2°

4°

• SETTLEMENTS

ISLANDS

REEFS

500 m
1000 m
3000 m
5000 m

0 kms   100   200
0 miles   50   100

BANABA
(OCEAN
ISLAND)

169°32' East of
Greenwich

0°53 S

Tabiwa

80 m △   Bitakonikai

Home
Bay   Ooma

Sydney
Point

0 kms   2
0 miles

JAPAN

NORTH PACIFIC

International Date line

MIDWAY

HAWAIIAN
ISLANDS

Hawa

MARIANA
ISLANDS

2°

MARSHALL
ISLANDS

CAROLINE
ISLANDS

BANABA
(OCEAN
ISLAND)

GILBERT
ISLANDS

PHOENIX
ISLANDS

Equator

NAURU

LINE
ISLANDS

NEW
GUINEA

SOLOMON
ISLANDS

TUVALU

SAMOA

FIJI

AUSTRALIA

NEW
CALEDONIA

TONGA

SOUTH

Tasmania

NEW
ZEALAND

West of Greenwich 174°

McKEAN
ISLAND

P   H   O   E   N   I   X

GARDNER
ISLAND

10

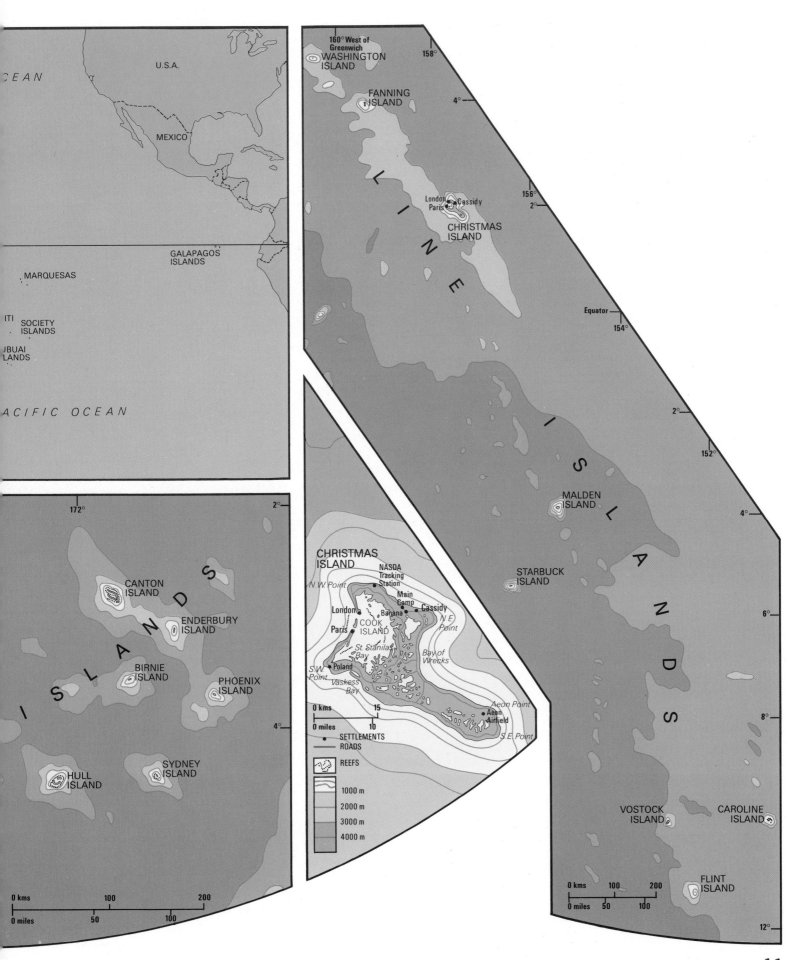

OCEAN

U.S.A.

MEXICO

GALAPAGOS
ISLANDS

MARQUESAS

ITI
SOCIETY
ISLANDS

UBAI
LANDS

ACIFIC OCEAN

160° West of
Greenwich
WASHINGTON
ISLAND
158°

FANNING
ISLAND
4°

L I N E

London Cassidy
Paris
CHRISTMAS
ISLAND
156°
2°

Equator
154°

2°

152°

I
S
L
A
N
D
S

MALDEN
ISLAND

STARBUCK
ISLAND

4°

6°

8°

VOSTOCK
ISLAND
CAROLINE
ISLAND

FLINT
ISLAND

12°

172°
2°

CANTON
ISLAND
S

ENDERBURY
ISLAND

I
S
L
A
N
D
S

BIRNIE
ISLAND
PHOENIX
ISLAND

4°

HULL
ISLAND
SYDNEY
ISLAND

0 kms 100 200
0 miles 50 100

CHRISTMAS
ISLAND
NASDA
Tracking
Station
N.W. Point
Main
Camp
London Banana Cassidy
Paris Poland COOK N.E.
ISLAND Point
St. Stanilas
Bay Bay of
Wrecks
S.W.
Point Poland
Vaskess
Bay
Aeon Point
Aeon
Airfield
0 kms 15 S.E. Point
0 miles 10
• SETTLEMENTS
ROADS
REEFS
1000 m
2000 m
3000 m
4000 m

0 kms 100 200
0 miles 50 100

"In the beginning there was nothing in the Darkness and the Cleaving Together save one person: We know not how he grew or whence he came. We know not his father or his mother, for there was only he. His name was Na Areau te Moa-ni-bai (Sir Spider the first of things). He walked over the face of heaven, which was like hard rock that stuck to the earth. And the heaven and earth were called the Darkness and the Cleaving Together.

So Na Areau walked over heaven alone: he trod it underfoot; he felt it with his hands; he went north, he went south, he went east, he went west, he fetched a compass about it; he tapped it with the end of his staff; he sat upon it and knocked it with his fingers. Lo, it sounded hollow as he knocked, for it was not sticking to the earth below. It stood forth as the floor of a sleeping house stands over the ground. And none lived below in the hollow place, nay, not a soul, for there was only Na Areau. So he entered beneath that rock that was heaven and stood below.

And now is Na Areau about to make men grow beneath that rock; he is about to command the Sand to lie with the Water, saying, 'Be ye fertile'. They heard; they brought forth children, and these were their names: Na Atibu and Nei Teakea.

Then Na Areau commanded Na Atibu to lie with his sister Teakea. They heard; They brought forth children and these were their names: Te Ikawai (the eldest), Nei Marena (the Woman Between), Te Nao (the wave), Na Kika (Sir Octopus), Riiki the Eel, and a multitude of others".

From *Migrations, Myth and Magic
from the Gilbert Islands*
ROSEMARY GRIMBLE

Introduction

The Gilbert Islands are a chain of coral atolls which are scattered across the central Pacific and comprise the Gilbert Islands, the Phoenix Islands and the Line Islands, all today grouped as the single national entity of the Gilbert Islands. Tarawa, the capital, is situated near a point where the Date Line meets the Equator. The total land area is about 260 square miles, but the thirty-three islands are spread over approximately two million square miles of ocean. Except for Banaba (Ocean Island), which rises to a height of 265 feet above sea-level, all the islands are low and narrow, sometimes as little as one hundred yards wide.

The climate of the Gilbert Islands group is dominated by the Pacific Ocean. Both temperature and rainfall vary little throughout the year. The south-east trade winds help to keep the land cool and maintain the temperature at about 80°F. August and September are the driest months, the wettest are December and January. The wind will occasionally blow from the west or north-west, often bringing squalls and heavy rainstorms. All the islands sometimes suffer from drought, particularly the Southern Gilberts.

The Gilbertese are of mixed Micronesian and Polynesian descent and speak one language, which is common to all the islands. It is not known exactly when the Gilbert Islands were first inhabited, but it is generally held that there was a migration by a race of people who came from the west (south-east Asia and particularly Indonesia has been suggested) in about 300 AD. Only some of these invaders settled; the main body moved southwards through Tuvalu and Rotuma to Samoa. In about 1200 AD the Samoans attacked their enemies, the descendants of the invaders, and expelled them. They scattered in many directions, but a large number returned along their original route and, on arriving once again in the Gilbert Islands, they fought their ancestral kin and settled permanently there. Much of their history is recorded in the legends and traditions of the present-day Gilbertese. The islands, though separated by open sea, developed a strikingly similar social order and a unity of tradition, broken only in the north, and there, only in the nineteenth century.

The European discovery of the Gilbert Islands dates from the sixteenth century. It is thought that Christmas Island and Nonouti were sighted in 1537 by Grijalva's mutinous crew on their disastrous voyage across the Pacific to New Guinea. Quiros is reported to have seen Butaritari in the Northern Gilberts in 1606. After these probable early Spanish sightings, further discovery had to await the latter part of the eighteenth century and the first quarter of the nineteenth century. After Captain Byron's visit to Nikunau in 1765, the remaining twenty-four islands in the group were discovered largely as an unintended result of increasing commercial activity in the Pacific. The last islands to be discovered were Onotoa and Beru in 1826. From 1823 onwards the waters of the Gilbert Islands became favourite sperm whaling grounds and the crews occasionally deserted and settled there. Trading ships began to visit the islands regularly from 1850, and some of the "beachcombers" became respected residents, traders and agents for trading firms in Australia, America and Germany. Although, at first, trade merely consisted of bartering curios for European luxuries, trade in coconut oil began about 1860 and in ten or twenty years gave way to the sale of copra.

Largely between 1860 and 1870, slave-traders raided many of the islands, carrying away islanders to the South American guano mines and coffee plantations, and to Fiji, Tahiti, Hawaii and Queensland. The Gilbertese are said to have resisted the slave-gathering fiercely and there are accounts of several ships being destroyed and the crews slaughtered by the local inhabitants.

The introduction of Christianity followed soon after the first traders had established themselves in the islands. Dr. Hiram Bingham of the American Board of Foreign Missions landed at Abaiang in 1857 and with the help of Hawaiian pastors began to spread Christianity through the northern Gilbert Islands. In 1870 the Reverend S. J. Whitmee of the London Missionary Society carried Christianity to the Southern Gilberts and placed Samoan pastors at Arorae, Tamana, Onotoa and Beru. The Society continued to spread northward and in 1917, by agreement, the American Board withdrew from the country handing over to the London Missionary Society, which has itself now withdrawn in favour of the Gilbert Islands Protestant Church. In 1888 Fathers Bontemps and Leray of the Sacred Heart Mission landed at Nonouti. Catholicism is still established throughout the Gilbert Islands with the exception of the most southerly islands, which are still Protestant strongholds. By 1900 an expedition had been sent by the Pacific Islands Company to Banaba and a concession was obtained to mine the rich phosphate there.

The Gilbert Islands became a British protectorate in 1892 and a crown colony in 1916. In 1941–1942 the Japanese occupied some of the Gilbert Islands, but were ejected in 1943 by the American forces. The US marines' victory in the Battle of Tarawa against a heavily defended position set the pattern for the subsequent American domination of the Pacific. In 1975 the eight former Ellice Islands became the new state of Tuvalu and the rest of the Gilberts proper, the Northern Line Islands and the Central and Southern Line Islands, remained part of the Gilbert Islands. The split came as a result of a referendum which was held towards the end of 1974, in which the overwhelming majority of the Ellice people voted in favour of separation. Internal self-government for the Gilberts was granted on 1st January, 1977 and Independence was fixed for July 1979.

The encroaching influence of outsiders—whalers, traders, missionaries and administrators—inevitably effected changes in the traditional pattern of Gilbertese life. A gradual acceptance of Christian codes meant that some traditions and practices were *either prohibited or fell into disuse. However, the* maneaba *has remained central to the life of the Gilbertese people.*

The local community meeting house, or maneaba, *used to be the focal point both of political and social life in each village and each island.* Mane *means to collect or bring together and* aba, *the land or the people of the land. There are traditions of magic, strict procedure and skill associated with the construction of a building of such importance to the Gilbertese community. The meetings of the elders were held there and they discussed all matters concerning the life of the village and there, too, were held the games, communal feasts and dances. Complex traditions were maintained and it was also a place where people of the neighbourhood would meet, simply to relax and chat. The political powers of the* maneaba *system have passed to the elected members of the national House of Assembly. Each island elects one or more members by secret ballot and the "House" then selects a number of candidates from whom the Chief Minister is chosen after a further national election. He then appoints his own ministers.*

It is significant that the Gilbertese name for the House of Assembly is maneaba ni maungatabu. *Today, the* maneaba *is still essential. The Gilbertese culture endows the old with special dignity and authority so meetings of the* unimane *(old men) held in the* maneabas *are still of importance in deciding village matters and in upholding rules of behaviour. There is no heated discussion in the* maneabas; *an individual will complete a strong eloquent monologue and immediately be seated. The extended family matters very much to each person and the obligations of this sense of community dominate life. Maneaba decisions are made through an intricate process of consultation, and the belief that everyone should be kept informed about the details of ordinary life is important. The* maneaba *today is also a place for public meetings, wedding feasts, films and dances.*

Dancing is very much part of traditional Gilbertese entertainment. At most feasts or special occasions there is dancing, when with great pride dancers will display their skill and the old people will relive the memories of the dances and stories of their youth. The movements of the dancer portray the words of the accompanying song. Young dancers begin their training at about four years old, as soon as they can understand the directions they are given. Each village has a man or a woman who is expert in teaching the formal movements of the dances. Dancing is very much a family and community affair, people of all ages sharing the struggle for perfection of movement and the emotions of the performance. New songs of important events or emotions are always being written and performed alongside dances from generations past. In this way the old and the new can be heard and preserved.

Land tenure in customary law, which has been codified, does not permit unrestricted right of disposal. Tenure is in the form of a life tenancy and the registered owner is rather in the position of a trustee for his family. Traditionally each plot of land, which is a thin strip stretching across an island, is marked by coral stones sunk deep into the ground. A landowner is bound to allow his children to obtain a livelihood from his land. The estate of the registered owner must pass to his next of kin on his death, although he has limited powers to dispose of certain lands by sale, gift or exchange during his lifetime. This customary law of inheritance has led to excessive subdivision, which situation is inevitable on islands with a growing population and few alternative means of livelihood. Those who seek sources of employment elsewhere usually return home so that others may enjoy a short period of affluence. All islanders are thus basically dependent on their land.

Although the islands are remote from the centres of industry and power and the soil poor and thin, sustaining only a limited number of plants, the people enjoy affluent subsistence living and their adaptation to a specialised environment is remarkable. The sea, the coconut and the pandanus provide the necessities for food, travel and shelter.

Much of the Gilbertese food is eaten raw, but cooking is done by the women over open fires. For feasts and special occasions, the food is cooked in an earth oven which is a bowl-shaped hole in the ground lined with hot stones on which food is left to cook, covered over with matting. The diet consists of fish including turtles, shark, octopus, eels, sandworms and shellfish, and also coconut, pandanus and babai, which may be considered the staples, and fruit, such as pawpaws and bananas. Pigs and chickens are kept for feasts. A variety of puddings and sweetmeats are created from toddy syrup, coconut and babai.

Coconut and pandanus trees provide the materials for the supports and thatch to build a Gilbertese house. Even the sennit string which lashes the whole structure together is obtained from the coconut husk.

The Gilbertese canoe plays an important role in providing transport, food and sport and is almost entirely built from coconut and pandanus trees. After an increasing number of accidents and loss of lives, inter-island canoe travel was banned by the Government, except between a few islands which are close to each other. The traditional baurua, a large ocean-going canoe up to a hundred feet in length and owned by a village, is no longer built; although there has been a recent revival of interest after James Siers' adventurous passage from Tarawa to Fiji in a baurua, specially built in the village of Taratai on North Tarawa. The Gilbertese canoe is perfectly suited for fishing around the islands and sailing the quiet waters of the lagoon. It is amongst the fastest in the Pacific. There are a number of designs, that range from the long narrow racing canoes with enormous triangular sails to short deep fishing canoes which are paddled. The construction of a canoe is the work of a skilled craftsman and each important stage of the building is marked by feasting and celebrations. Skills of *building, trim and the magic associated with its construction are closely guarded family secrets.*

The traditional economy and way of life for many Gilbertese was altered by the discovery of phosphate in Banaba and Nauru (a separate island state north-west of Banaba). Apart from the export earnings of the phosphate, nearly every Gilbertese family has experience of some relative working either in Banaba or Nauru and they have thus become accustomed over several generations to travelling outside their own islands for work. The people have applied their sea-going tradition to employment on modern ships. Banaban phosphate is a wasting asset which will be exhausted by the end of the 1970s. The export earnings will then depend on copra (of which about 10,000 tons is exported each year), remittances from seamen and workers in Nauru and the advent of a commercial fishing industry, which is seen as the mainstay of the future.

The Gilbertese generally wear Western-style dress in cotton materials. However, they prefer to go barefoot and men will only wear long trousers on formal occasions, preferring shorts or lava-lavas (loose sarongs). They wear shirts for going to church or an event which demands comparable solemnity. Women also wear lava-lavas and usually stibuta *or bodices, which are in bright primary colours. On any important occasion, such as a departure or arrival of an honoured guest or for a celebration like a birthday, people wear a flower wreath and the garlanding of visitors is the start of any ceremony.*

There is a duality in the Gilbertese people which superficially seems perplexing to outsiders. Although shy with strangers, they are fluent and often outspoken orators, with a deep love of singing and uninhibited dancing in the maneabas. *They are gentle and generous to guests, but fierce protectors of their lands and traditions; solemnity explodes readily into laughing fun, natural dignity exists alongside skilful and often hilarious mimicry in a people committed to Christianity, who are also acutely aware of ancient and traditional beliefs.*

The same contrasts are evident in the present-day development of society in the Gilbert Islands. The characteristics of the Gilbertese people, their sense of fairness, their sense of humour, their respect for knowledge gained by experience and their commitment to freedom of speech and majority decisions will be formative elements as the Gilbert Islands establishes its place in the world of independent nations.

18

Chapter 1
THE ISLANDS

*"If one draws a circle around the island world of the Pacific, at
its centre will be found the perfect models of the South Sea
Islands of romance: a necklace of sixteen low coral atolls
straddling the equator and almost touching the 180th meridian.*

*These are the Gilberts; where Melville found his Mardi and
Stackpole his exemplar of the blue lagoon. Lost in an immensity
of ocean they are blessed with a superb climate, pleasantly warm
without humidity, tempered by the constant bracing trade
winds, and inhabited by the friendly and lovable Micronesian
people . . ."*

From the Foreword by H. E. Maude
to *Astride the Equator*
ERNEST SABATIER

The island of Marakei is an example of an atoll whose reef completely encloses a lagoon.

Above: *a reef platform.*
Left: *jagged coral channels fringe the reef.*
Opposite: *a causeway will link the island of Bairiki with Betio which can be seen in the distance.*
Overleaf: *a lagoon at low tide.*

Left: *sailing on the lagoon.*
Below: *a* kainakotari *or local latrine.*
Bottom: *the lagoon shore is made of fine coral sand.*

A coral road and coconut palms.

Left: *a germinating coconut.*
Above: te ing, *the hessian-like fibre near the top of the coconut tree.*
Right: *the coconut tree provides food, shelter and transport.*

Above and above right: *young and mature pandanus or screw pine trees.*
Right: *the fruit of the pandanus can be eaten raw or cooked.*
Opposite: *pandanus leaves.*

Far left: *pawpaw.*
Above: babai. *Rotting vegetation is wrapped in a basket of pandanus leaves and placed around the bottom of the stem to feed the plant. The roots are an important food for special occasions.*
Left: *the flower of the babai.*

43

Left: *breadfruit is spiked on the midrib of a coconut frond for easy transport.*
Below: *breadfruit trees are planted for food, but they also provide shade for the villages.*

46

Left: *a village house.*

A boy shelters in a maneaba from the torrential rain.

Left: *regular users of Co-op shops, found throughout the Gilbert Islands, become members of a branch and receive a small annual refund.*

Left: *the entrance to Betio harbour projects into the lagoon. The ferry, Nei Nimanoa (top) was built at the shipyard there. All the copra from the Gilbert Islands is stored at Betio harbour (above) before being shipped overseas.*

58

Left: *welding pontoon pipes for use in the construction of the new causeway.*
Above: *containers on Betio wharf awaiting lighterage.*

Below: *legacies of World War II are to be seen on Betio, the site of the Battle of Tarawa.*
Right: *motorbikes are a popular form of transport on most islands.*

Below: *an air service connects many of the islands.*
Right: *the approach to Cassidy airport, Christmas Island.*

Christmas Island has several seabird colonies of worldwide scientific importance, with eighteen species nesting regularly on the main island and lagoon islets. The majority of species are protected by law and three areas—Cook Island, Moto Upua and Mota Tabu—have been designated bird sanctuaries with restricted access.
Left: *a colony of* kiriri *or sooty tern.*
Below: *a* matawa *or white tern.*
Bottom: *an eitei or frigate bird, which is a national symbol and features prominently in the poetry, dance and songs of the Gilbertese.*

A tinebu *or Christmas Island shearwater.*

A moukena *or blue-faced booby.*

An international jet service links Tarawa
to Christmas Island, Honolulu and Nauru,
from where connections can be made to
Australia, Fiji and Hong Kong.

The satellite tracking station at Christmas Island.

Chapter 2
THE PEOPLE

"It began to dawn on me that beyond the teeming romance that lies in difference between men—the diversity of their homes, the multitude of their ways of life, the dividing strangeness of their face and tongues, the thousandfold mysteries of their origins— there lies the still profounder romance of their kinship with each other, a kinship which springs from the immutable constancy of man's need to share laughter and friendship, poetry and love in common. A man may travel a long road, and suffer much loneliness, before he makes that discovery. Some, groping along in the dark byways, never have the good fortune to stumble upon it. But I was luckier than most. The islands I had chosen blindly, for the only reason that they were romantically remote, were peopled by a race who, despite the old savagery of their wars and the grimness of their endless battle with the sea, were princes in laughter and friendship, poetry and love . . ."

From *A Pattern of Islands*
ARTHUR GRIMBLE

72

By tradition, the maneaba, or meeting
place is central to the life of each village.
Today it is still the focus of most
communal activities—village council
meetings, dances, shelter for strangers
and film shows.
Right: family representatives meet at
their maneaba.

78

When a soft sponge is washed up on the beach, it is collected to make pillows.

Above: *food is usually cooked outside or in small open kitchens.*
Right: *collecting well water. Rain seeps through the sand forming a layer of potable water on top of the underground sea water.*

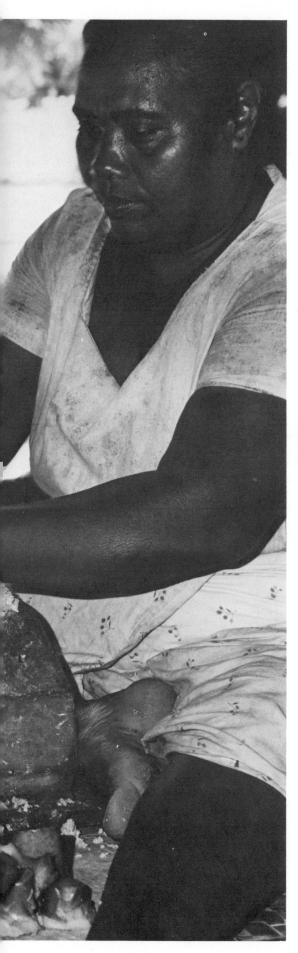

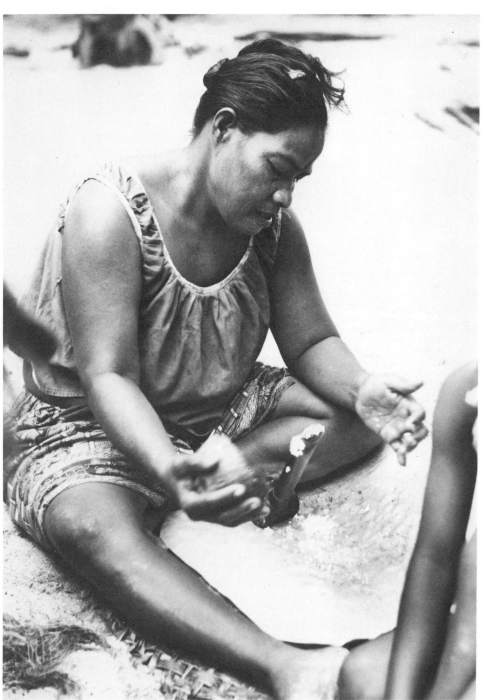

Left: *grated* babai *is the basis of* te bekei,
a sweet dish.
Above: *a coconut is grated, in this
instance, on part of a bicycle frame.*

Above: kamaimai, *the syrup from boiled toddy, is added to the grated* babai *and the mixture is wrapped in* babai *leaves before boiling.*
Right: tarabuti *are threaded on the midrib of a coconut frond, before being cooked.*

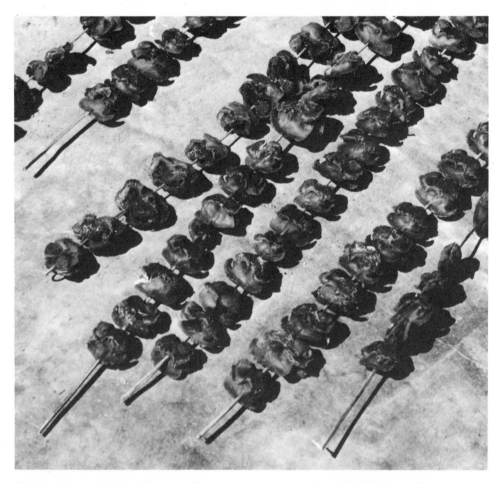

Above: *drying te bun. These small shellfish are spiked on coconut fronds, which are often used as skewers.*

Right: *cooking fish. Traditionally a fire is made in a small hollow and covered with te bun shells. The fish are wrapped in parcels of woven coconut fronds and placed on the shells. They are covered with coconut husks and allowed to cook for several hours.*

Returning home with firewood.

Above: *basket weaving.*
Right: *a family shares a meal of*
te koumara *or small shellfish.*
Overleaf: *a few families own sewing*
machines, which are borrowed when
needed by others, a practice known as
bubuti. *Most clothes are made at home.*

By skilful cutting morning and night, the spathe of the coconut tree produces toddy or coconut sap, a drink which is rich in vitamins. It is drunk fresh or boiled and mixed with tea. If allowed to ferment, it becomes powerfully alcoholic.
Left: trees that are regularly tapped for toddy have steps cut into their trunks.

Left: *a man will often collect toddy from a number of trees.*
Above left: *shaving the spathe of the coconut tree.*
Above right: *toddy runs down the leaf which is specially inserted into the end of the spathe and thus collects in coconut shell containers.*
Overleaf left: *toddy containers drying overnight after being washed.*
Overleaf right: *an empty beer bottle used to collect toddy.*

Copra, the dried kernel of the coconut, is
one of the main exports of the Gilbert
Islands. Between five and ten thousand
tons are shipped each year to Europe,
where it is processed to make vegetable oil.
Left: collecting the debris from coconut
trees for fuel.
Top: the kernels of coconuts are spread
out to dry in the sun.

Above: *prising the kernel from the shell.*
Right: *selecting coconuts for copra.*

106

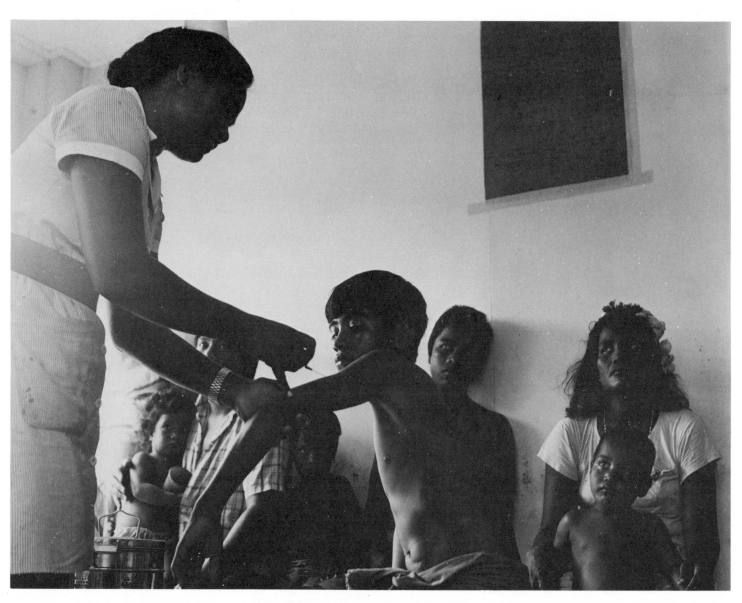

Out-patients at Tungaru Central Hospital.

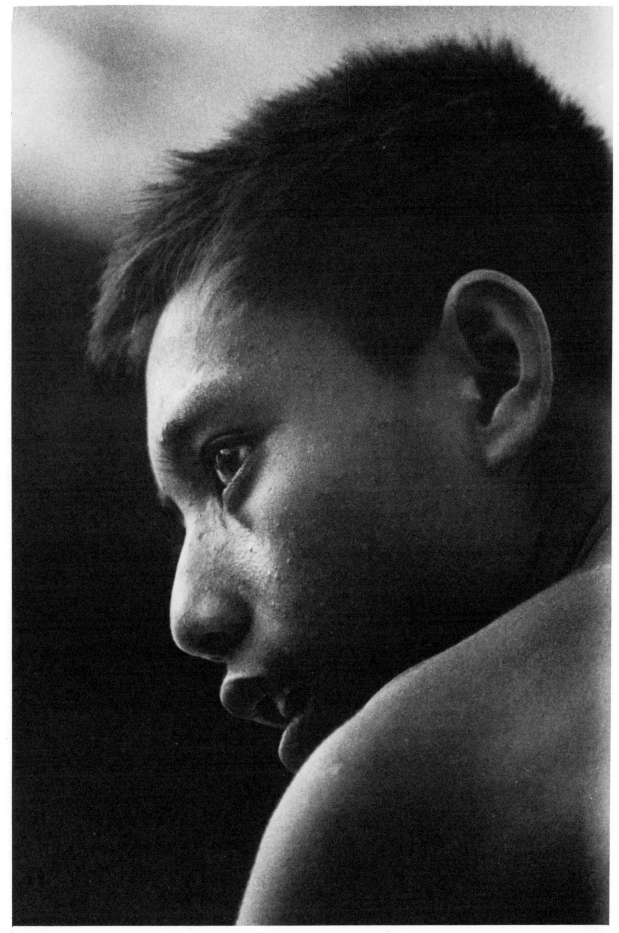

South Tarawa is served by privately owned buses.

110

Above: *the* T.S. Teraaka, *the Gilbert Islands' training ship.*
Opposite top: *students attending practical workshop instruction at the Marine Training School.*
Opposite below: *dockers at Betio.*

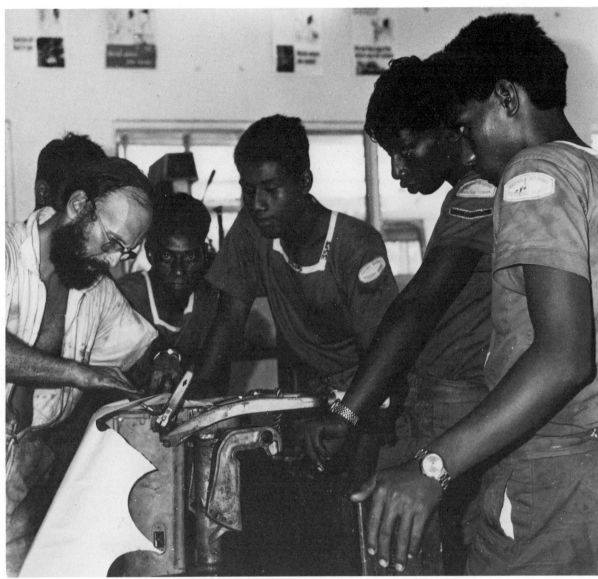

113

114

Guitars and ukeleles provide the rhythm for popular Gilbertese songs.

Above: *broadcasting from Radio Tarawa.*
Opposite top and bottom: *a local pop group, which travels to other islands by boat.*

117

Above: te oreano. *The object of this game is to throw the ball powerfully at the opposing team and a point is scored if that team fails to catch it.*

Right: te ano. *The ball used in this game is traditionally made by wrapping te ing, the hessian-like material from the coconut tree, around a good-sized stone. When the wrapping is thick enough, it is held together with a tight mesh of coconut string. To add extra weight, the ball is soaked in the sea and can weigh over 12 lbs.*

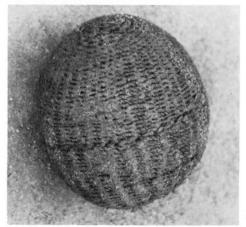

Below: te boiri. *This game is played with a cube ball, seen to the right of the bottom picture, which is made from woven pandanus. The game can be played competitively in teams or individually just for fun. The object is to keep the ball in the air, kicking it with the side of the foot. The players clap in time with the kicking to add to the excitement.*

Opposite: *volley ball is a popular game throughout the islands.*
Left: Naubwebe, *the mythical father of string figures, demanded that all souls passing to the afterlife should perform a series of figures. This is the first.*
Below: Naumake *is the second stage, which is about to be developed into the third by the second player. There are probably more recorded figures or games in Micronesia than in any other region in the world.*

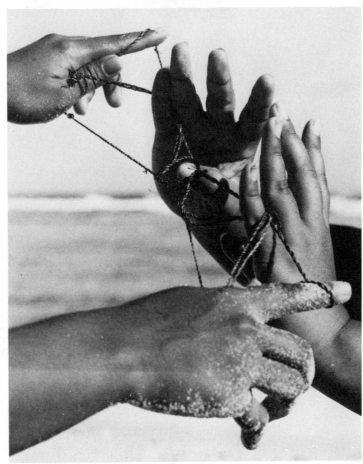

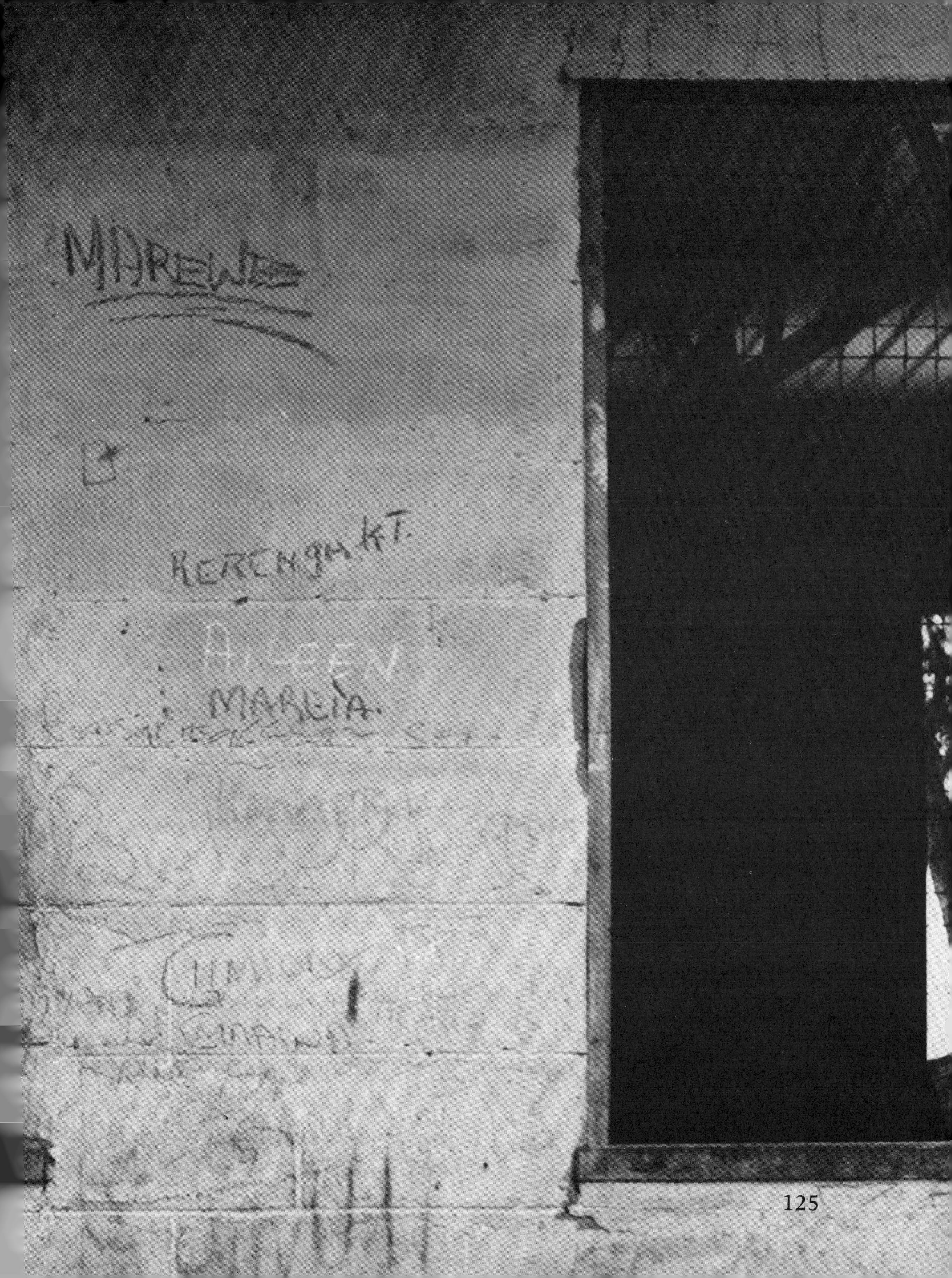
RERENGA K.T.
AILEEN
MAREIA.

132

Left: *nearly all Gilbertese are Christian—divided almost equally between Catholic and Protestant faiths.*

Below: *an old woman makes an offering at her grandfather's shrine.*

*Graves are now frequently edged with
bottles and strewn with broken glass.*

Chapter 3
BUILDINGS

"The houses were of all dimensions, from those of toys to those of churches. Some might hold a battalion, some were so minute they could scarcely receive a pair of lovers; only in a playroom, when the toys are mingled, do we meet such incongruities of scale. Many were open sheds; some took the form of roofed stages; others were walled and the walls pierced with little windows. A few were perched on piles in the lagoon; . . . no nail had been driven, no hammer sounded, in their building, and they were held together by lashings of palm tree sinnet."

From *In the South Seas*
ROBERT LOUIS STEVENSON

Left and preceding page: *as many as three thousand pieces of thatch are needed to roof a medium-sized* maneaba. *Many of these roofs are supported by large slabs of coral* (seen above and right) *which is also used in house construction.*

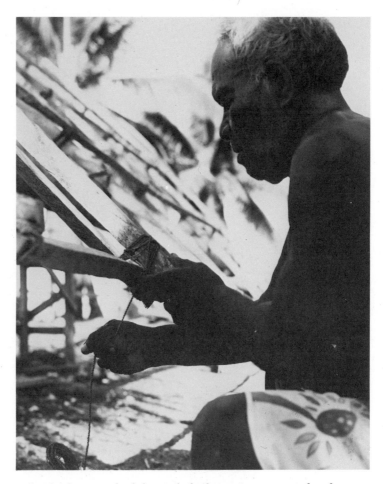

Left: *the framework of the roof of a house is constructed and thatched at ground level and lifted into position when complete.* Above: *roof timbers are lashed together with coconut string.*

*The spiky centre and edges of pandanus
leaves are removed in preparation
for weaving.*

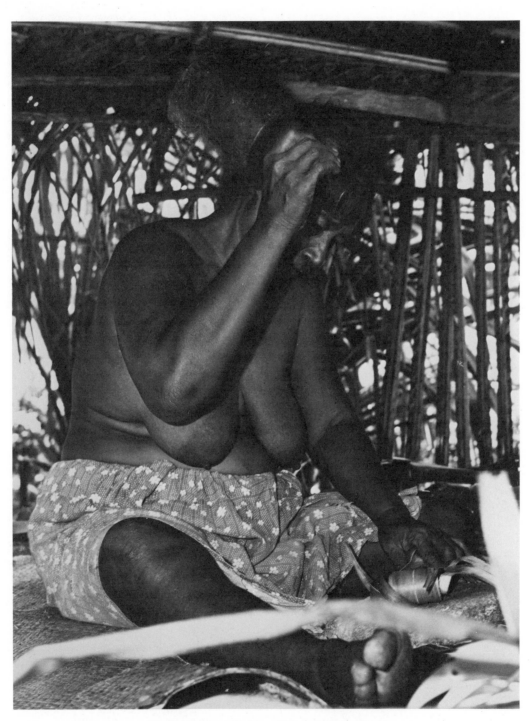

Each pandanus leaf is rolled and beaten to make it flat and pliable.

Right: *the pandanus leaf is cut into strips* with te bwere (seen above) *for weaving.*

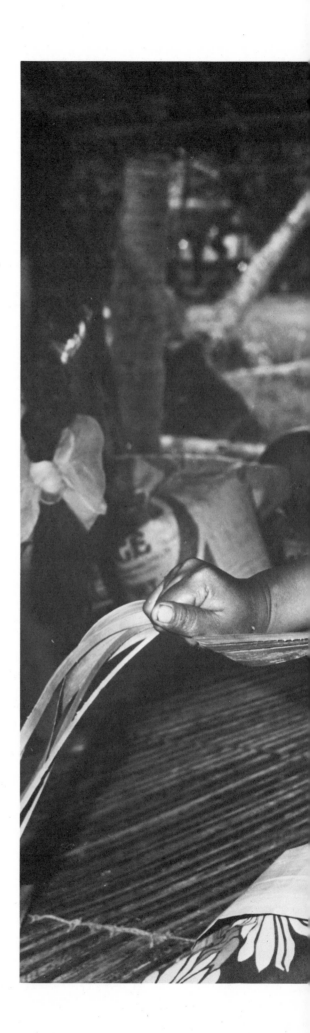

146

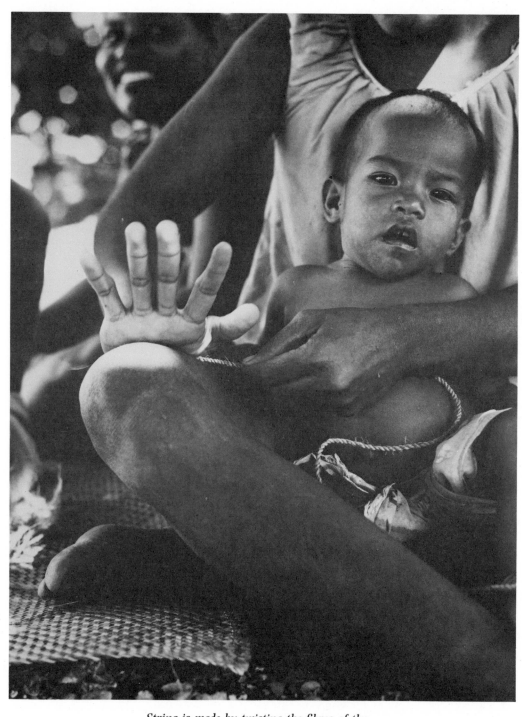

*String is made by twisting the fibres of the
coconut husks together and rolling them
along the thigh.*

*The pandanus leaf can also be pulled
around a stake to flatten it.*

The flattened leaves secured by the centre spine of the coconut leaf are wrapped over the midrib of the coconut frond; the thatch is attached to the roof framework.

152

The individual pieces of thatch are sewn on to the roof supports.

153

Above and right: *weaving mats from coconut fronds.*

Left: *a two-storey house.*
Above: *a bathroom.*

Above: *many people prefer a modern corrugated iron roof because it can be used to collect rain water and needs little maintenance.*
Right: *bus windows and wood from packing cases have been ingeniously incorporated into this traditional design.*

Left: *the House of Assembly on Tarawa
is the seat of Government in the
Gilbert Islands.*
Top: *modern buildings at Bairiki display
roofs based on traditional designs.*
Above: *houses built for
Government employees.*

*Walls are made by hanging mats on
lengths of coconut twine.*

162

Chapter 4
FISHING & CANOES

"The Gilbertese also handles his canoe with great skill. Anyone who has built his own canoe, who often fishes in it using a dragnet and who races with it, becomes one with it, rather like a rider and his horse. He loves and appreciates his canoe as if it were alive. Apart from its help in bringing in fish, it gives him other pleasures. Through it he experiences the intoxication of speed. When it skims over the smooth lagoon waters, sail at an angle and outrigger just out of the water, he knows the same sensation as a flier or a bird caught up in a high wind. There is the same dizzy thrill and rush of fresh air."

From *Astride the Equator*
ERNEST SABATIER

Left: *most of the work is done with simple tools, such as the adze shown here.*
Above: *an unfinished canoe.*

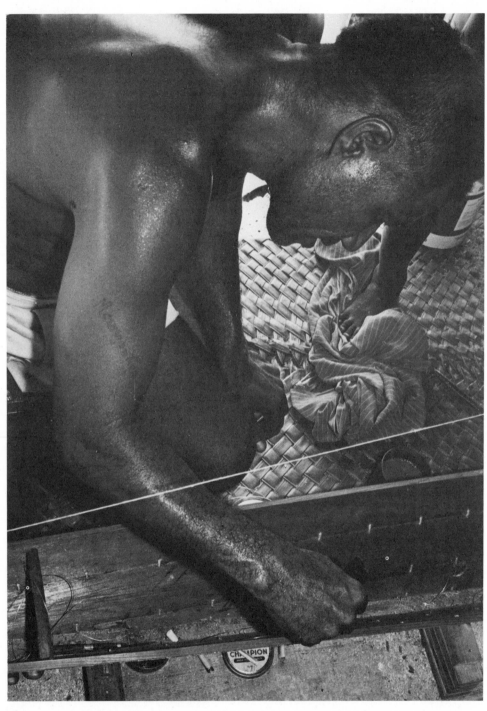

Above: *the craftsman does not use any glue, but relies on his skill to match the planks exactly for a perfect seal. Hull planks are tied into place before being sewn together.*

Right: *a temporary shelter is erected beside a craftsman's house and a canoe is built inside it.*

Above left: *the outrigger of a canoe.*
Above: *the hull of the Gilbertese canoe is long and slender.*
Right: *a sail dries in the evening sun.*

Scoop net fishing in the reef channels is done by beating the water with a palm frond to drive the fish along the channels into nets.

174

Below left: te bun, *small shellfish are collected at low tide in the lagoon* below *and sometimes stored in small stone circles close to the lagoon shore,* right. *The bottom picture shows net fishing in the lagoon.*

178

Opposite: *arrow-shaped fish traps are built from coral slabs.*
Below and bottom: *brine shrimp production on Christmas Island.*

The experimental fish farm at Ambo on South Tarawa has demonstrated the feasibility of intensive fish culture in atoll conditions. Vast intertidal areas in the lagoons can be converted into fish ponds. On Tarawa the cultivation of milk fish for use as live bait is being developed.

Above: *rod and line fishing from the reef edge.*
Right: *small fish are usually killed by biting the backs of their necks.*

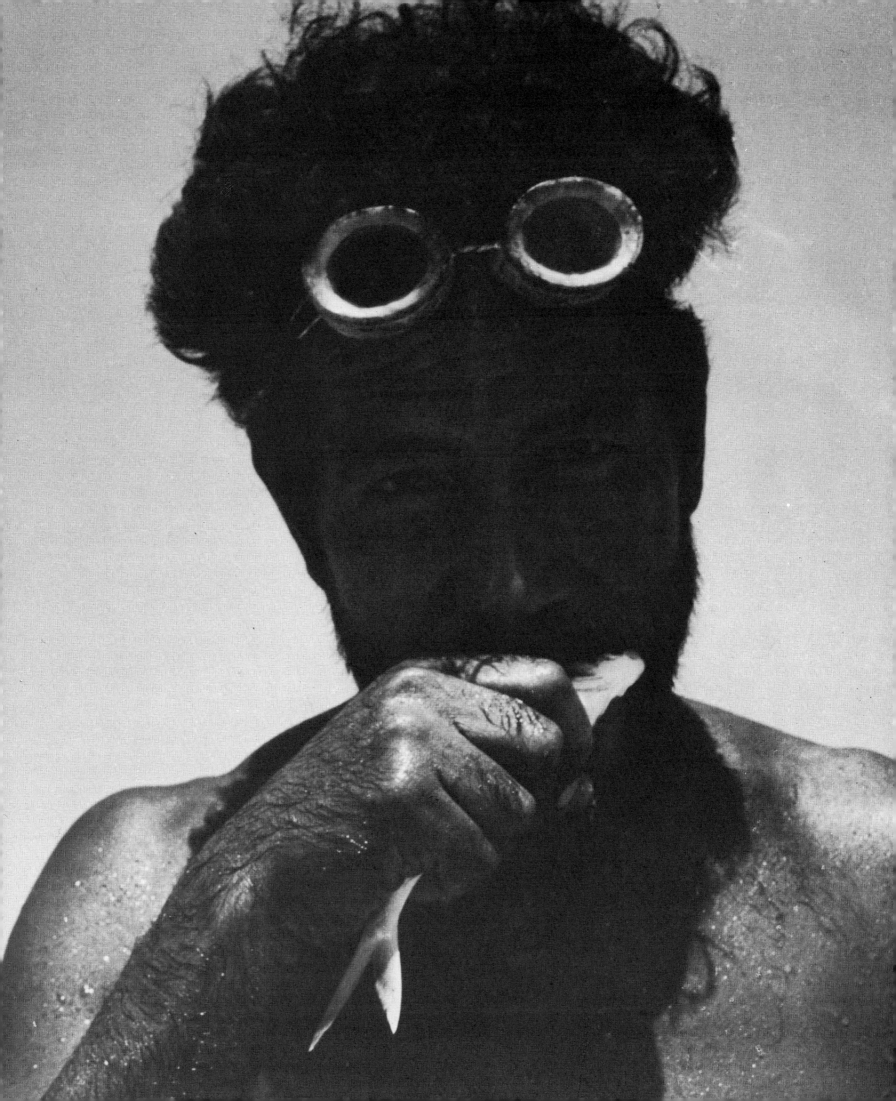

Above: *fish of all sizes can be caught by the ocean side using a simple strong line.*
Centre: *a small octopus is used as bait to lure prawns from their holes. They are netted when they try to return.*

The reef edge can easily wreck a canoe, so skill, judgement and experience are necessary to negotiate the surf.

Top: *bottom fishing in the lagoon.*
Above and right: *pond-bred bait is thrown
from the boat creating a feeding frenzy
amongst the skipjack, which snap wildly
at the fishermen's unbaited hooks.*
Overleaf: *by night, a burning palm frond
is used to attract flying fish, which are
then netted.*

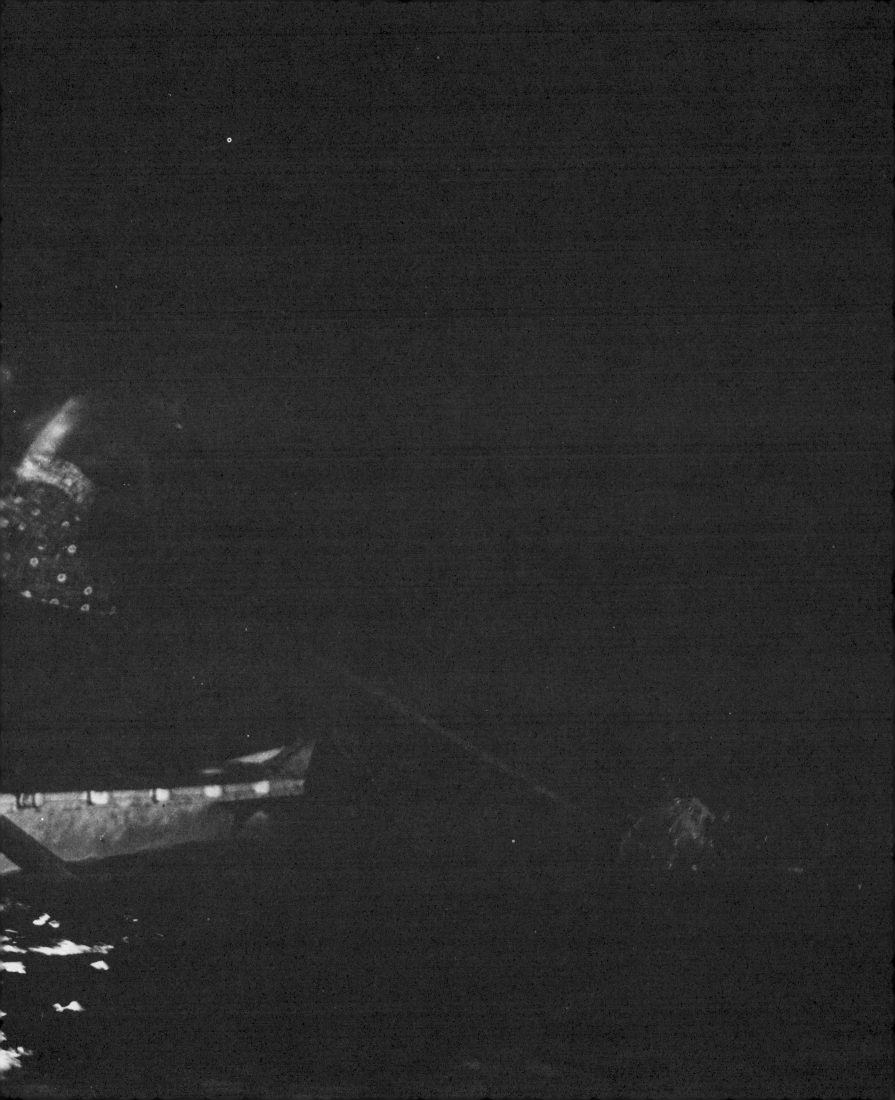

Left: *the fisherman returns home, heavily laden with the day's haul.*
Below and centre: *an eel trap.*
Bottom: *fish drying in the sun.*

Right: *returning from spear fishing at the reef edge.*

194

1

2

4

5

196

3

Overleaf: *the hull of the canoe is slightly asymmetric to allow for heel when the outrigger is raised.*

6

1 *A small fishing canoe sets sail in the lagoon.*
2 *Raising the sail.*
3 *Spars are made fast.*

4 *and* **5** *To tack, the sail is passed from one end of the canoe to the other; a skilful sailor lets the wind carry the weight.*
6 *The outrigger balances the sail and the crew must be alert to every wind change.*

Above: *the canoe can carry huge loads in the still waters of the lagoon.*

Top: *sails, sometimes made of flour bags, are measured to determine the class in which each boat should race.*
Above: *a canoe shed, in which small canoes are stacked under a large canoe's outrigger.*
Right: *lining up to race.*

Chapter 5
DANCING

"Slowly, on the low notes, the singing begins . . . then the pitch goes up and the pace speeds up too. Gradually the dancers warm up. At first they simply move their feet on the spot, waving their arms to follow the rhythm. They slap their hands on their bare chests, or on dancing mats covering their thighs. For the time being the women and the children don't imitate them, but they are the ones who sing with most abandon and who speed up the rhythm. Dancing on the spot and clapping their hands they urge the dancers to a paroxysm of movement. Nerves are tense, faces contorted and the voices become wild while the eyes grow haggard . . . Now the dancing is no longer on the spot: the semi-circle advances and retreats and then in an even more frenzied burst the finale is reached . . . Such a flood of passion is let loose and it is so infectious that even a man of another race has difficulty in calming his nerves and can hardly prevent himself from quivering in ecstasy with the rest of the audience and the dancers."

From *Astride the Equator*
ERNEST SABATIER